Sweet Swaddlekins

4 Easy Cloth Doll Patterns for Swaddle Baby Dolls

Great Beginner Sewing Patterns from Peekaboo Porch

Copyright 2018 Peekaboo Porch

www.PeekabooPorch.com

A Division of Peachy Keen Products

Sweet Swaddlekins

Patterns Included:

Swaddle Baby: Cuddly 8" Swaddle Baby First Doll Pattern with permanently attached blanket includes 9 different faces and 9 different hairstyles. All variations are included in this pattern. Combine the hair and face patterns with your favorite fabrics or fabric scraps and colors in any way you choose for endless possibilities!

Piggy in a Blanket: Cuddly 8" Piggy in a Blanket Baby Animal Swaddle Baby Doll Pattern with permanently attached blanket includes 3 different piggy faces for both boy and girl piggies. All variations are included in this pattern. Combine with your favorite fabrics or fabric scraps and colors in any way you choose and create YOUR favorite pig in a blanket!

Swaddlekins: Adorable, sweet Swaddlekins are a unique Swaddle Baby Doll Pattern with poseable arms and a permanently attached blanket for hours of baby doll fun. Pattern has 10 different faces and 6 hair choices for a total of 60 variations! Blankets can be made with a washcloth in this pattern to make them even quicker and easier. Combine with your favorite fabrics or scraps and colors in any way you choose and create your very own unique Swaddlekins.

Froggy in a Blanket: Cuddly 8" Froggy in a Blanket Baby Animal Swaddle Baby Doll Pattern with permanently attached blanket to make both boy and girl frogs. Blankets are made with a washcloth in this pattern to make them even quicker and easier. Combine with your favorite fabrics or fabric scraps and colors in any way you choose and create YOUR favorite frog in a blanket! This is a great beginner sewing pattern for cloth animal dolls! Hop to it and start making your Froggy Swaddle Baby Dolls today. :o)

Sweet Swaddlekins

A Book of 4 Easy to Sew Swaddle Baby Doll Patterns

Welcome to Peekaboo Porch where designing and making cloth rag dolls is our passion. There are 4 original swaddle baby patterns included in this book. We also list all the supplies needed at the top of each pattern for your shopping convenience. Swaddle baby dolls are also a great way to use up those beloved scraps of fabric and trim to make a creation that will last for years to come.

The Swaddle Baby is the easiest pattern and they progress in difficulty to the Piggy, then Swaddlekins and next Froggy. Each pattern is complete in its own section with step-by-step directions including diagrams and pictures of finished dolls. In addition, if you run into any difficulty while creating your doll please feel free to drop us a line or ask us a question by emailing peekabooporch@gmail.com Also, feel free to copy the pattern pieces from the book for your own personal use as many times as you would like.

Swaddle Baby dolls are great fun to make and allow your creativity to flow with all the variations included with the patterns and of course all of the endless possibilities of fabric combinations! With over 30 different doll designs be sure to check out all our patterns on Amazon or visit us at www.peekabooporch.com

We hope you enjoy creating dolls with our patterns as much as we enjoy sharing them with you. :o)

Peekaboo Porch Doll Patterns Are So Much Fun, You Can't Make Just One!

Happy Sewing!

Peekaboo Porch

Easy Cloth Doll PDF Patterns

1017

Swaddle Baby Doll Pattern

WELCOME TO PEEKABOO PORCH

Come On In and Create with Us...

SWADDLE BABIES

Cuddly 8" Swaddle Baby First Doll Pattern with permanently attached blanket includes 9 different faces and 9 different hairstyles. All variations are included in this pattern. Combine these hair and face patterns with your favorite fabrics or fabric scraps and colors in any way you choose for endless possibilities! Great beginner sewing pattern for cloth dolls. These Swaddle Baby Dolls are just like potato chips...You can't make just one! :o)

Swaddle Babies

Cuddly 8" Swaddle Baby First Doll Pattern with permanently attached blanket includes 9 different faces and 9 different hairstyles. All variations are included in this pattern. Combine these hair and face patterns with your favorite fabrics or fabric scraps and colors in any way you choose for endless possibilities! Great beginner sewing pattern for cloth dolls. These Swaddle Baby Dolls are just like potato chips…You can't make just one! :o)

Materials:
- 12-inch x 12-inch scrap of fabric for blanket
- 4-inch x 8-inch scrap of fabric for baby's head
- Embroidery thread or fabric markers for face
- One yard of 1-inch wide ribbon to bind blanket edge
- Choose one for hair:
    - Scrap of yarn
    - Scrap of felt or fleece
    - Scrap of silky curly fleece (available at Jo Ann's Fabrics)
- Optional trims of your choice:
    - Ribbons for hair bow
    - 8 inches of 1-inch wide gathered lace for bonnet
    - 4 x 4-inch fabric scrap for boy's bandana
    - 8 x 8-inch of blanket material for hat
    - 2 small black beads for open eyes
- Polyester fiberfill

Directions:
1. Cut out head pieces

2. Cut 12-inch x 12-inch square of fabric for blanket

3. Choose your face

Face: To transfer face to doll, lay face pattern down on head pattern on right side of material and pin in place. Using a sharp pencil, twirl pencil through paper, making tiny dots to transfer face.   Remove paper and lightly join dots with pencil to draw face to embroider.

If you are adding embroidered top curls, trace these now. If you are using markers, draw the face now.

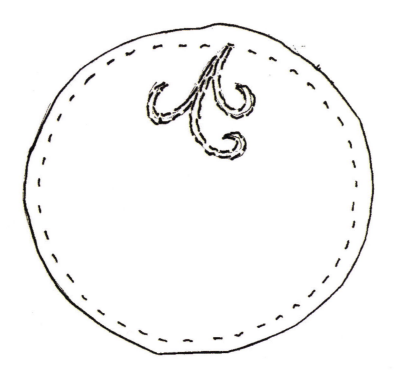

Embroider or paint

Note: If you are using beads for eyes, they must be sewn on <u>after stuffing</u> to make them more secure.

4. Sew around head, leaving open between X's.   OR, if you prefer, you can sew all the way around the head and cut a one-inch slit on back side only.

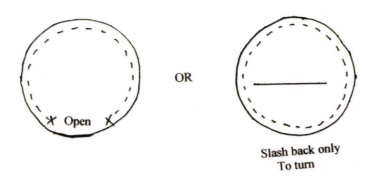

Slash back only
To turn

Clip all around head and turn right side out. Stuff head and stitch opening closed by hand. Do not be concerned about how this looks as it will not be seen when doll is finished.

If embroidering face or hair, do it now. If you are making the Raggedy Ann baby, the nose may be embroidered or you may slip stitch a red felt triangle from face pattern in place. If using beads for eyes, sew securely in place after stitching in the eyelashes. You may embroider the eye circles, which is preferable for children under 3.

Ears: To finish ears, make running stitches by hand, up and back down where ear meets head.

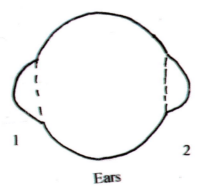

Ears

5. Choose your hair:
To use yarn, choose one of the following options:

- Loop yarn from seam, tacking in place at seam and arranging loops to end above eyes and ears and then tack ends of loops in place.   This works really well on boys. It also looks really good on girls with a hairbow, especially if you use any kind of fuzzy looking yarn.

Looped Yarn

- <u>For curls all over doll's head</u>, wind yarn over two fingers in a figure 8 pattern, leaving 3-4 loops on each finger. Do not cut yarn. Slip off, and with matching thread, tack to head where yarns crossed. Repeat until you have all the curls you want.

Yarn Curls

- <u>For baby topknot</u>, just make one set of loops like above and tack at top of head where yarn crossed on the figure 8 loops. This leaves half of loops standing up for topknot. Arrange remainder of loops on forehead and tack in place. Sew hairbow at center of loops.

Yarn Topknot

- <u>To use felt or fleece or any non-raveling material</u>, cut from pattern. Sew top seam, clip and turn. Slide on doll's head. If needed, you can push a little stuffing inside wig, and then slip stitch in place with matching thread. If you like, you can cut a narrow strip of fabric and loop it at center hairline for a little curl or you can use a scrap of matching yarn for a curl and tack securely in place. Or, you can cut front slits for bangs and tack in place in front.

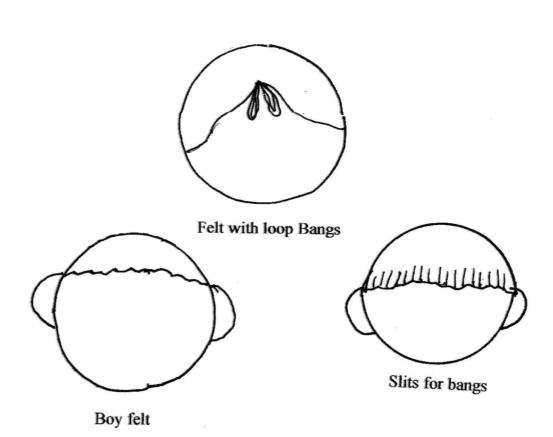

Felt with loop Bangs

Boy felt

Slits for bangs

- <u>Silky Curly Fleece</u> (available from Joann's Fabrics) makes a really nice head of hair. Cut strip from pattern and by hand, turn under all four sides ¼-inch.   This will keep the fabric from raveling. Start at one side of the head (below ear level for girl and top of ear level for boy) and sew to head all the way across to the other side. Sew short side back. Sew other short side toward back.   Run a gathering thread on remaining long side, pull up and tack to back of head. Do not worry about how this looks; the back of the head will not be seen on the finished doll.

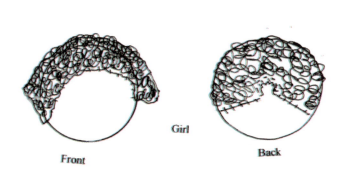

Silky Curly Fleece

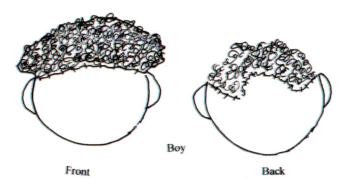

Additional Options:

<u>For lace bonnet</u>: Tack gathered lace in place from below ear line across head to other side. Gather cut ends of lace and pull up and tack in place.

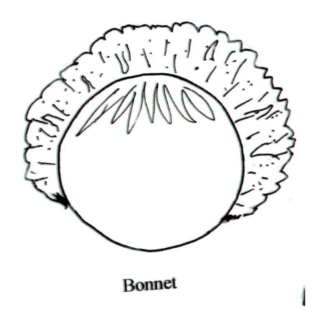

Bonnet

<u>For headband</u>, use strip of lace. For rosette, gather 2-inch long piece of lace on one side and pull it up to make rosette. Add bow in middle if you wish.

Rosette

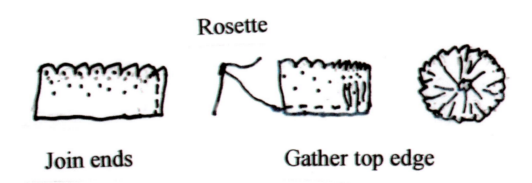

Join ends   Gather top edge

<u>For boy's bandana</u>: Fold; stitch all sides, leaving open between X's. Clip; turn; press. Hand stitch opening closed and tack in place AFTER you sew head to body.

<u>For long hat</u>: Sew seam. Hem hat edge and tack in place on doll's head.

Lay completed doll head to one side.

6. <u>Blanket</u>: Fold blanket square to make triangle; then fold again to mark center. Mark with pin.

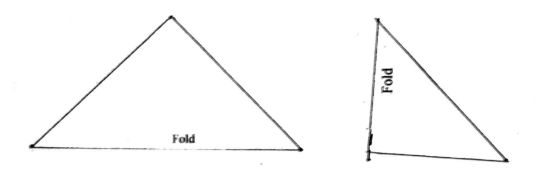

Open blanket. On paper or cardstock, trace the body pattern guide piece and pin to blanket, matching center notch to the pin on the blanket.   Pin this paper guide in place and sew at both edges to the top. Backstitch, then sew at paper edge.

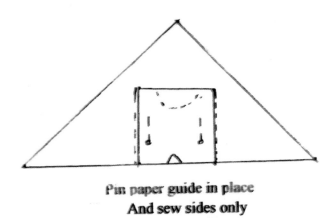

Remove paper pattern and stuff the pocket, forming the body. Then sew top of body closed.

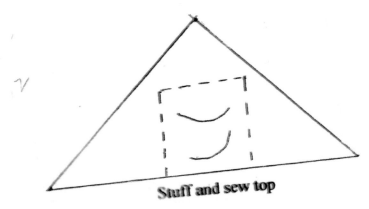

To sew head to blanket: Turn down top point of blanket and insert needle in seam into the body only.

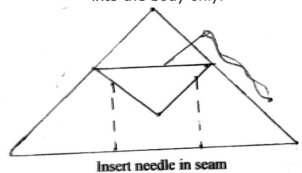

Lay blanket top up and place head on body, overlapping as shown on body guide pattern. Doll is cuter if head is tilted slightly and not perfectly straight. Sew in place firmly, side to side.

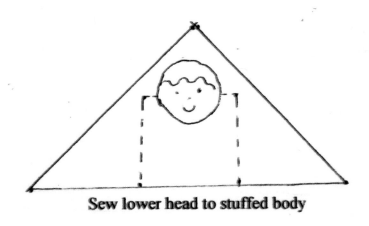

Sew the rest of the head to blanket corner, making sure you attach it to the top of the blanket only. Sew firmly all of the way around the head.

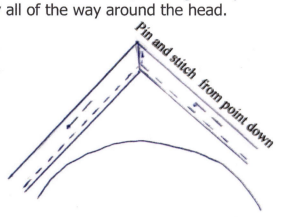

Backstitch bottom edge and trim excess ribbon from both sides.

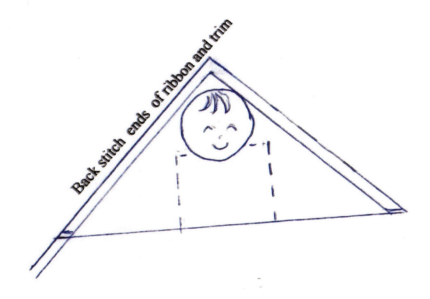

Your new Swaddle Baby is now ready to be wrapped, cuddled and loved! Enjoy. :o)

Turn the page to look at all the variations you can make with just this one pattern. Don't you want to make another one?

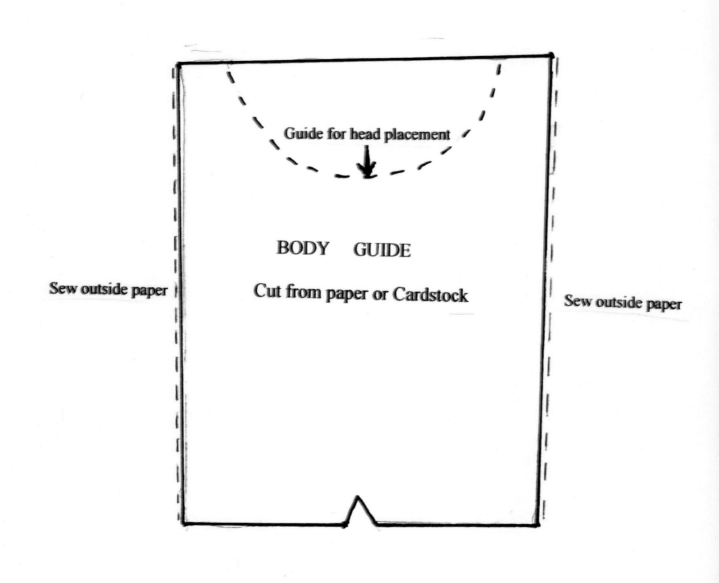

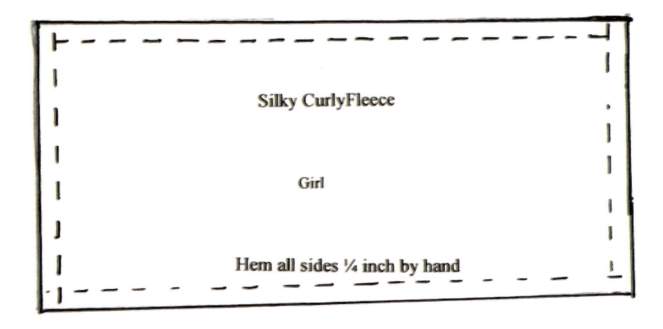

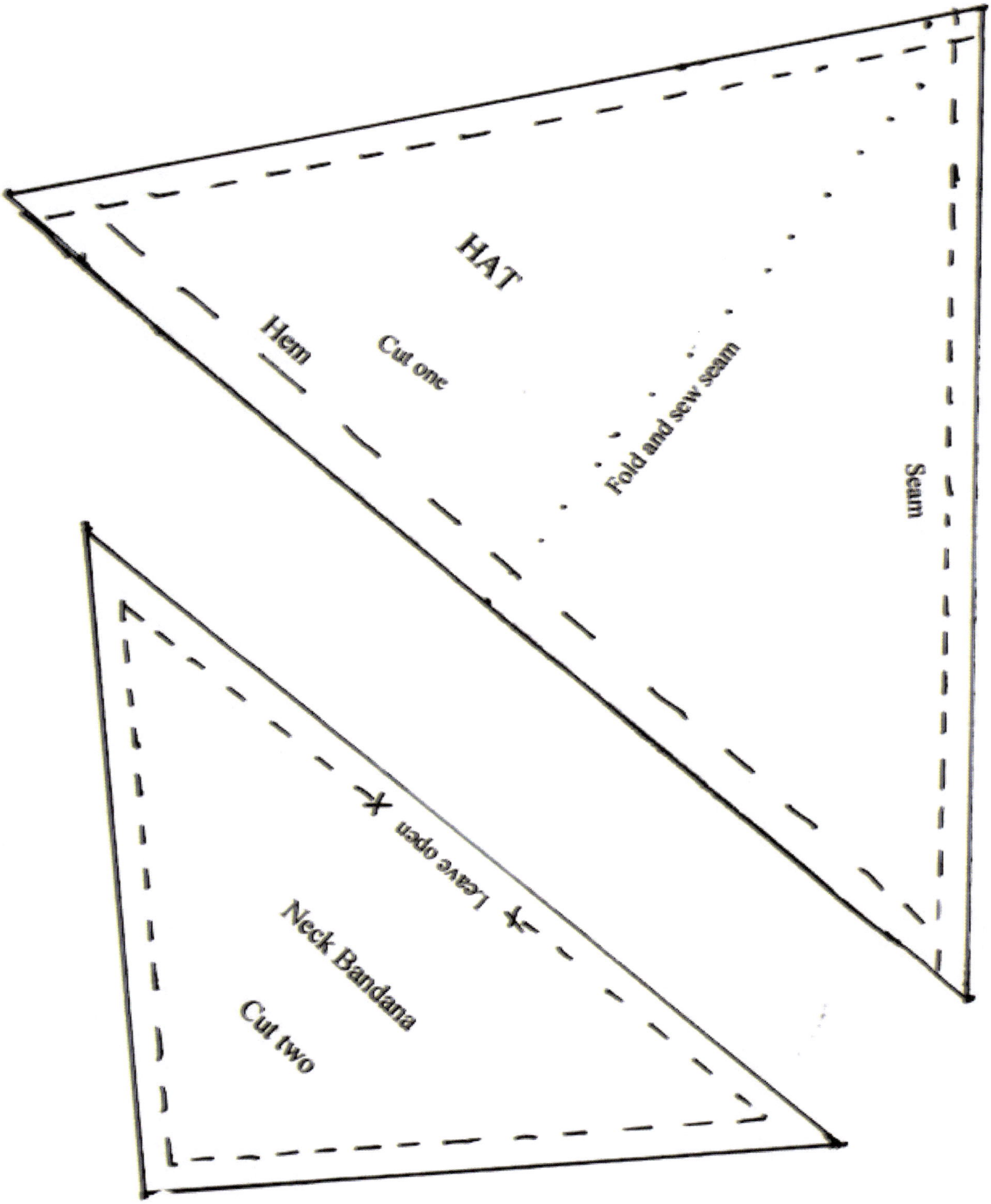

HAT
Cut one
Hem
Fold and sew seam
Seam

Neck Bandana
Cut two
Leave open

Choose Hair

Use this pattern for felt or fleece hair.
Also use for the base of the Raggedy Ann hair made of silky, curly fleece.

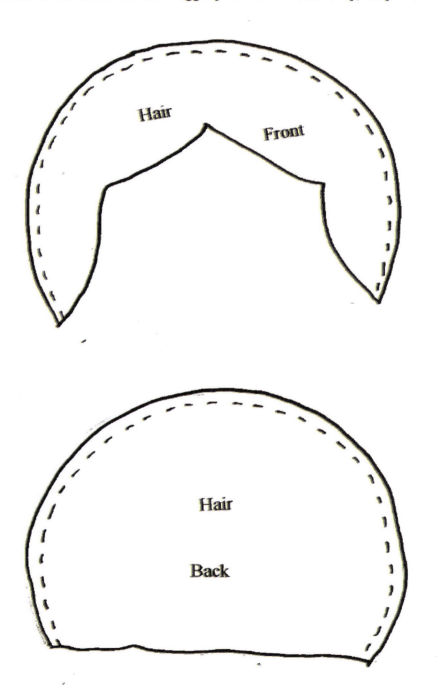

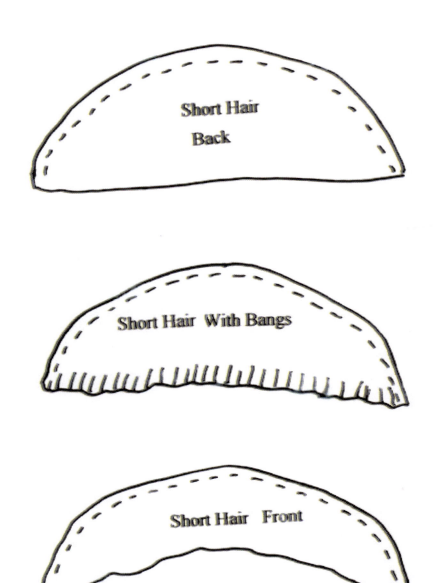

Choose your hair

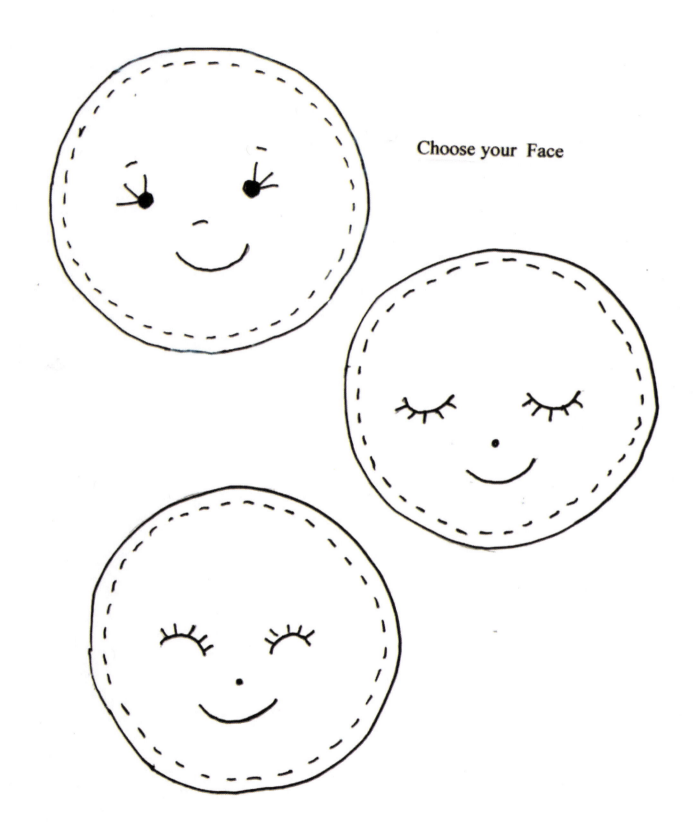

Choose your face

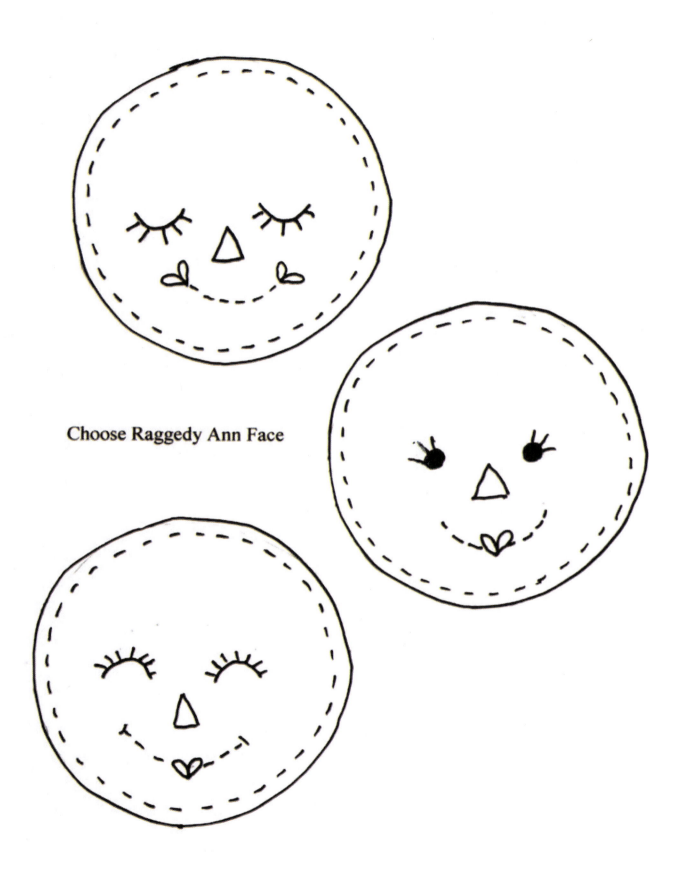

Choose Raggedy Ann Face

Peekaboo Porch
Easy Cloth Doll PDF Patterns

1018

Piggy in a Blanket Swaddle Baby Doll Pattern

PIGGY IN A BLANKET

Cuddly 8" Piggy in a Blanket Baby Animal Swaddle Baby Doll Pattern with permanently attached blanket includes 3 different piggy faces for both boy and girl piggies. All variations are included in this pattern. Combine with your favorite fabrics or fabric scraps and colors in any way you choose and create YOUR favorite pig in a blanket! Great beginner sewing pattern for cloth animal dolls. These Piggy in a Blanket Baby Animal Dolls are just like potato chips...You can't make just one! :o)

Piggy in a Blanket

Cuddly 8" Piggy in a Blanket Baby Animal Swaddle Baby Doll Pattern with permanently attached blanket includes 3 different piggy faces for both boy and girl piggies. All variations are included in this pattern. Combine with your favorite fabrics or fabric scraps and colors in any way you choose and create YOUR favorite pig in a blanket! Great beginner sewing pattern for cloth animal dolls. These Piggy in a Blanket Baby Animal Swaddle Dolls are just like potato chips...You can't make just one! :o)

Materials:
- 14-inch x 14-inch piece of fabric for blanket
- 12-inch x 18-inch piece of pink fleece for piggy's head and ears
- Embroidery thread– light pink for nostrils & dark pink for mouth
- Choose one for eyes: 2 small black beads for open eyes or brown embroidery thread for other eyes (Beads should not be used on Swaddle Babies for children under the age of 5 due to choking hazard)
- Choose optional trims of your choice:
    - ♣ Ribbons for hair bows
    - ♣ 8 inches of 1-inch wide gathered lace for bonnet
    - ♣ 4 x 4-inch fabric scrap for boy's bandana
    - ♣ 5 inches of lace for trim at neck of girl piggy
    - ♣ 3 X 4 inch fabric scrap for bow tie or hair bow
- Polyester fiberfill stuffing
- Quilting thread to attach head, snout and ears
- Blush for cheeks

Piggy in a Blanket

Directions:
1. <u>Piggy:</u> Cut out head, snout and ear pieces from pink fleece.

2. Using doubled quilting thread, run a gathering thread around the edge of the large pink yo-yo to make the Piggy head. Pull up thread to gather, leaving a quarter-sized opening. Stuff Piggy head with fiberfill. Pull gathering thread to tighten then sew criss-cross to close opening.

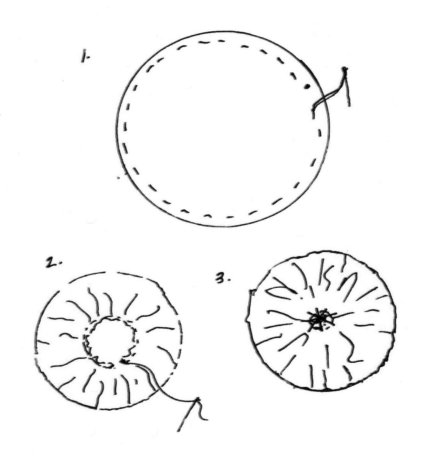

3. <u>Piggy Snout:</u> Repeat above instructions to make the yo-yo snout. Insert thread to front and make one straight stitch for each nostril. Return to back of snout, pull tight and knot. Using light pink embroidery thread, make one french knot in the center of nostril stitch. Using dark pink embroidery thread, make one stitch for mouth. If you want more of a piggy smile, make one tiny stitch in center of mouth and pull down slightly. Pin snout in place on head and attach with slip stitch.

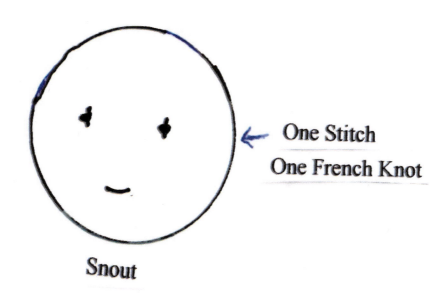

Snout

4. Sew beads firmly in place for eyes or embroider eyes of your choice.

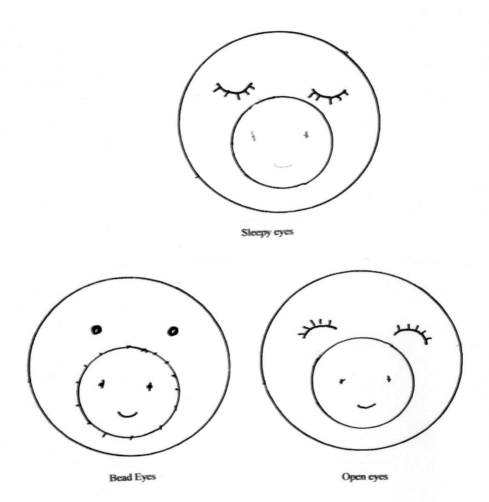

5. Pin ears in place with dotted line on ear pattern to the edge of head as shown. Sew the first ear on back of head. Sew only 3 sides to edge of head. Front of ear is loose so it will fold forward a bit and look natural. Overlap the second ear on the back as shown. If you want a lace bonnet, slip stitch the lace in place around the edge of the head now. Don't worry about how the back of the head looks, it will not show when finished.

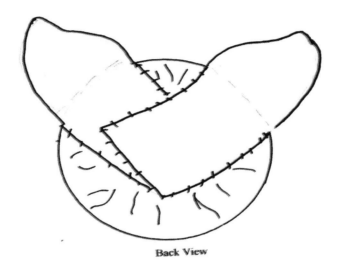

Back View

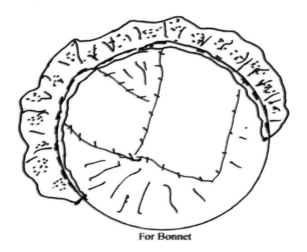

For Bonnet

6. <u>Blanket:</u> Cut 14 x 14 inch square for blanket and fold right sides together to form a triangle. Sew up 4 inches on each side as shown, leaving top point open. Clip and turn right side out and press. Also press down remaining seam allowance at point.

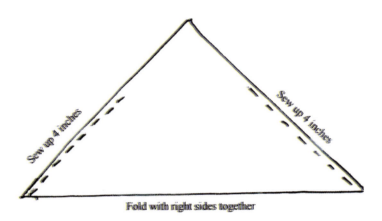

7. Fold and mark center at bottom edge of blanket with pin.

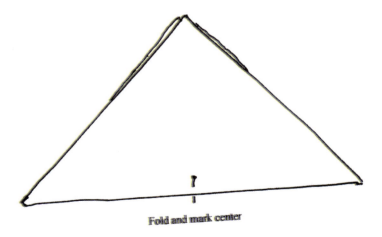

Copy and cut out the paper body sewing guide and match the notch to the pin on the blanket. Pin paper guide in place. Sew along the outside of the pinned paper pattern on both sides from edges to top and backstitch at each end.

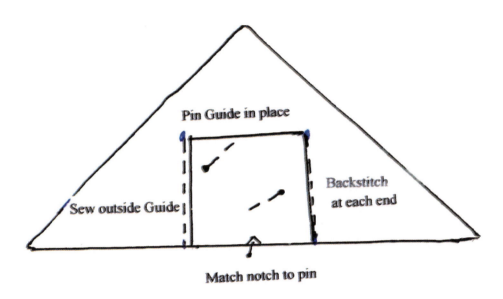

8. Stuff fiberfill in top opening of the paper guide to form body. Remove paper guide. Stitch top opening closed. If you want lace trim add it now along the top of stitching at top of body.

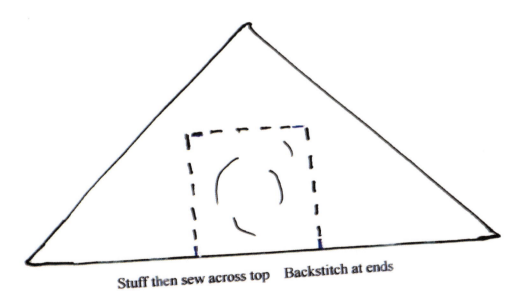

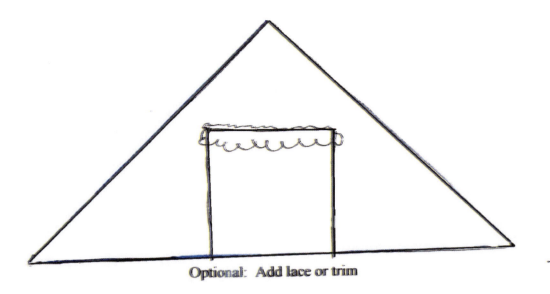

Optional: Add lace or trim

9. Place piggy head so chin overlaps the body about ½ inch as shown in front view. Pin in place on TOP blanket ONLY. Point of back blanket will be folded down as shown in back view. Hand stitch in place. Insert needle in back seam and secure lower part of face to body.

Front View   Pin head in place overlapping chin on stuffed body

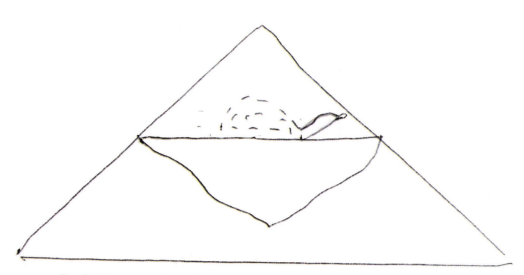

Back View   Stitch Head in place by hand on just one layer of blanket

Insert needle at seam and tack chin in place through stuffing

10. Topstitch edge of blanket closing the open point at the top as you go.

Top stitch edges of blanket

11. <u>Bow Tie or Hair Bow:</u> Fold and stitch edges leaving open between the x's on pattern. Clip, turn and topstitch all four sides. Press. Gather in center and tack to piggy at neck for a boy or to top of head for a girl's hair bow.
12. <u>Bandana:</u> Fold right sides together and stitch, leaving open between x's. Clip and turn. Press. Top stitch on sewn edges only. Tack end to body at side of pig's head leaving folded edge free at chin.
13. Brush powdered blush lightly inside ears and on cheeks.

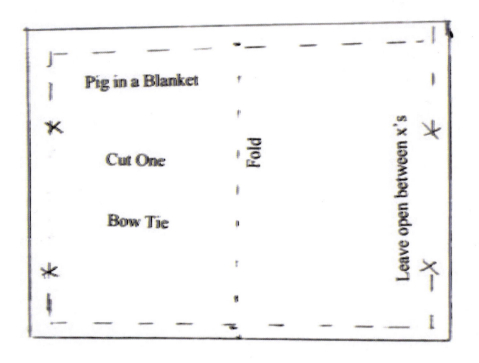

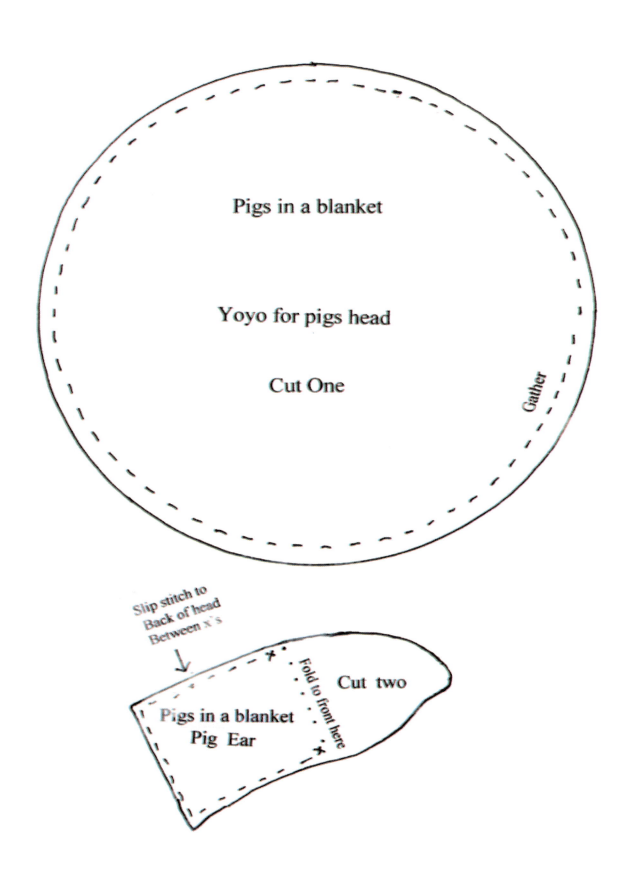

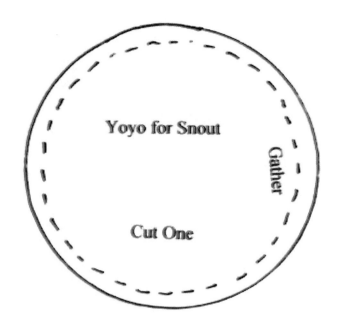

Yoyo for Snout

Gather

Cut One

Pig in a Blanket

Body Guide

Cut one from Paper

1020

Swaddlekins Swaddle Baby Doll Pattern

Come On In and Create with Us...

SWADDLEKINS

Swaddle Baby Doll with Poseable Arms & Multiple Variations for Hair and Face

Adorable, sweet Swaddlekins are a unique Swaddle Baby Doll Pattern with poseable arms and a permanently attached blanket for hours of baby doll fun. Pattern has 12 different faces and 5 hair choices for a total of 60 variations! Blankets can be made with a washcloth in this pattern to make them even quicker and easier. Combine with your favorite fabrics or scraps and colors in any way you choose and create your very own unique Swaddlekins.

SWADDLEKINS

Sweet little swaddle baby with moveable and poseable arms is all snuggly and warm in a permanently attached blanket. Mini size only 7 inches long is just right for little hands to hold. It's a great way to use up your scraps with this easy to make baby doll. For a quick version doll, you can just use a washcloth for the baby blanket.

MATERIALS:

6" by 6" fabric for doll head
9" by 12" fabric for pajamas

Blanket: Choose One:

12" by 12" fabric OR 1 washcloth

Hair: Choose One:

Embroidery thread
OR yarn
OR 3" by 6" scrap fo fleece for curls
OR 4 " of purchased fringe
OR 4" by 1" scrap of fleece for snipped bangs
OR 1 ½ " by 4" of silky curly fleece or furry fleece*
(*available at Fabric or Craft Store)

Embroidery thread for face or use 2 beads for eyes
(Beads should not be used on Swaddle Babies for children under the age of 5 due to choking hazard)
Polyester Fiberfill

For Optional Hats and Accessories:

Baby Bonnet: 6" scrap of gathered lace or gathered eyelet
Fabric Bonnet: 10" by 7" scrap of fabric
Cap: 6" by 6" fabric
Ball Cap with Bill: 6" by 9" scrap of fabric
Cap with Tassels: 6 " by 2" scrap of fleece Long
Nightcap: 7" by 7" scrap of fabric
Farmer Boy Hat: 4" by 8" scrap of fabric
Baby bib: 4" by 8" scrap of fabric
Farmer Boy Bandana: 5" by 5" scrap of fabric
Swaddle Baby Crib: One 6x9x2 Plastic Basket*
*(Available in organizing dept of most stores)

Directions:

1. Run Doubled gathering thread by hand around head and pull up leaving quarter sized opening.   Do not cut thread yet.

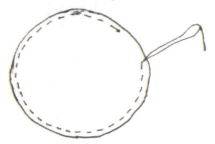 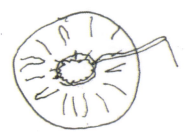

2. Push fiberfill into opening, firmly filling head. The eraser end of a pencil can be used to push fiberfill into head. Pull gathering thread up tight to close hole. Sew across numerous times, knotting repeatedly and closing hole.

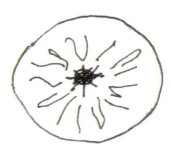

3. Mark face on dolls head. The easy way is to trace face on paper and pin to doll's head. Twist point of pencil at nose and eye dots, making a hole in paper pattern and leaving a dot on dolls for embroidered French knot or bead for eyes.   For smiles or curved eyes make a row of dots then remove paper and join dots with pencil, transferring face to fabric.

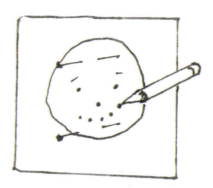

4. Use 2 strands rose embroidery thread for mouth. Make one French knot for nose. Open eyes are two French Knots or two beads. Use two strands of Black or Brown embroidery thread for sleeping or happy eyes.

5. CHOOSE YOUR HAIR STYLE

    Embroidered hair: Transfer pattern using above instructions and embroider.

    Using yarn or all six strands of Embroidery floss:

    <u>For bangs</u> make 3 to 7 loops. Tack on back of head then smooth forward.

    <u>For Topknot</u>   Make loops in a figure 8. Tack at top of head where the 8 crosses. Tack on hair bow.

Yarn Curls Wrap yarn around two fingers in Figure 8. Wrap 3 times on each finger. Slide off. DO NOT CUT YARN. Tack to head with matching thread in your needle' where 8 crosses beginning at side of head about even with mouth. Repeat all around face ending even with mouth on the other side. Cut yarn now.

Fleece Bangs Cut one from pattern and snip edges as marked on pattern. Tack to edge of cap before attaching hat to head.

Fleece Curls Trace Spiral Pattern on paper and pin to square of fleece, cut on lines following arrows. Tack end to side of head beginning level with mouth. Twist making a loop curl and tack to head. Repeat, ending level with mouth on other side, looping and tacking with matching thread as you go. If you need more curls cut another spiral.

Silky Curly Fleece or Furry Fleece   Cut pattern out on back side of fleece. Baste down all four sides with matching thread to stop shedding.   Pin center to top of fore head and tack in place around dolls face. Run doubled gathering along dotted lines on pattern at back of wig and pull up to fit head. Tack in place including sides.

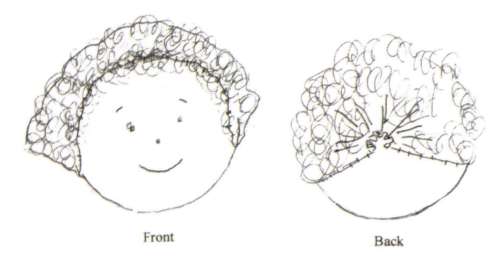

Front   Back

Fringe   Use 3" to 4" scrap of fringe and tack to edge of hat or cap before tacking hat to head.

6. OPTIONAL HATS:

LONG HAT:
Sew seams together. Hem edge. (If you are using fringe or fleece bangs tack them in place now.) Tack hat in place on doll with hat seam in back. If needed, gather back to fit head and hat to head.

CAP:
Fold with right sides together and sew ends. Turn right side out and press. (if you want fringe hair or Fleece bangs, tack to folded edge now. Slip stitch the folded edge to dolls head. Gather back edge, pull up to fit dolls head and slip stitch in place.

CAP WITH BRIM:
Sew ends, turn right side out and press. Sew bill, clip, turn and press. Pin bill to center front on folded edge of hat. Top stitch folded edge of hat securing bill in place. Tack hat on head around face.   Run gathering thread at back edge and pull up tight tacking to back of head.

FLEECE HAT WITH TASSEL TOP
Snip hat edge as marked on Fleece hat pattern. If using fleece bangs, slip stitch to front edge of hat.   Tack front edge of dolls hat around dolls face. Run gathering thread ¼ "

below the cuts on hat back edge and pull up tight,   Knot and tack hat to dolls head, tacking loose ends down.

LACE OR EYELET BONNET:
Tack a 4-5 inch scrap of gathered lace or eyelet around dolls face
Beginning about even with mouth and ending about even with mouth on the other side.
A flat scrap of wide lace can also be used the same way to make a little lace cap.

Back

FARM BOY HAT
Trace paper pattern and pin to 2 layers of fabric wrong sides together.   Sew around pattern and cut out leaving ¼ " edge.   OR
join 2 squares of fabric with fusible web and then cut out. Tack to back of dolls head.

Farm Boy Bandana Fold on dashed line with wrong sides together. Topstitch both sides leaving ¼ " raw edge.   After head is sewn on doll, slip stitch ends of bandana to sides of head.

FABRIC BONNET: Fold right sides together.   Sew ends, turn and press.   Begin at X and hand gather and ending at x .

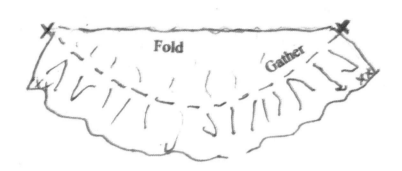

Pull up thread gathering to fit around dolls head. Folded edge is brim of bonnet. Tack bonnet to head on gathered thread line.

Hand gather edge from XX to XX pulling up to form hat. Tack in place on dolls head, also tacking ends down. This will not be seen when doll is finished .

Back

PAJAMAS:

7. Cut out a paper pajama pattern and cut out the slash on paper as marked.

Slash on BACK side of pajamas ONLY

Do not cut fabric yet. Fold fabric right side together, pin paper pattern on fold and mark slash on fabric BACK of pajama ONLY. Remove paper and cut slash on back of pajamas only.

Re pin pattern in place, matching slash on pattern to slash on fabric. Using pattern as a guide sew all around pajamas beginning>at bottom fold and ending at bottom fold.

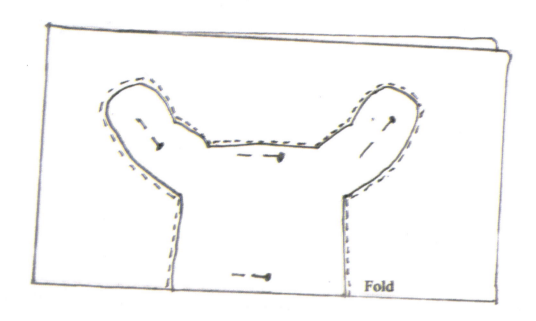

8. Cut out pajamas leaving ¼ " seam allowance. Carefully clip all curves

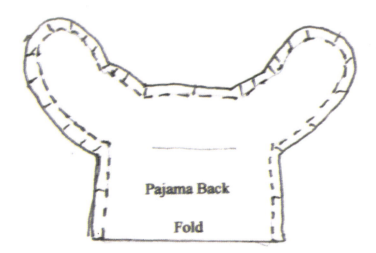

9. Turn right side out through slit in back. Use eraser end of pencil to push hands out. Press.

10. Using eraser end of pencil push stuffing into hands, stuffing to elbow only. This will allow poseable arms freedom to move.

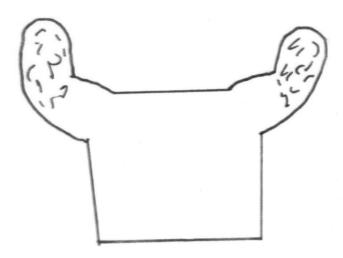

11. Optional Bib   With right sides together sew curved seam, clip turn and press. Center bib at neck under pajamas on side with slash with right side of bib down. Sew in Place. Press down to pajama front.

12. CHOOSE FABRIC BLANKET OR WASHCLOTH BLANKET

Fabric Blanket   Fold 12" by 12" square of blanket fabric into triangle with right sides together.   Stitch up 6 inches on each side, leaving a ½ " seam allowance, leaving point at top open.

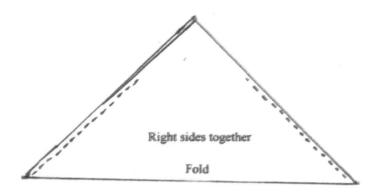

Clip seam. Turn right side out and press. Also press down ½ seam allowance on point

13. Wash Cloth Blanket: Fold forming triangle but do not sew.

14. For both fabric blanket and washcloth blanket versions, fold triangle and mark center with pin.

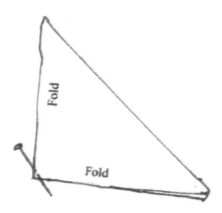

15. Thread sewing machine on top with thread that matches the pajamas.   Thread bobbin with thread that matches washcloth or fabric blanket.

16. Pin pajamas to blanket or washcloth matching pin with notch at center of pajamas SLIT SIDE DOWN,

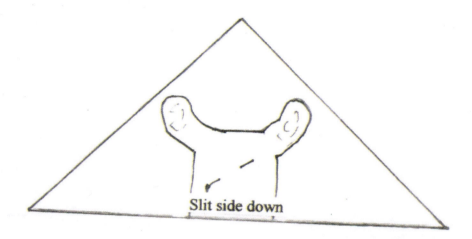

For bib version turn bib up.

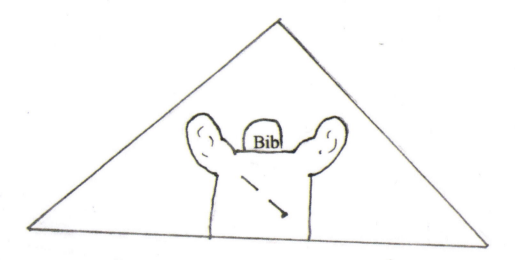

17. Starting at shoulder sew, following dotted lines on paper pattern, sewing to underarm, down side, across bottom, up other side and across to shoulder.

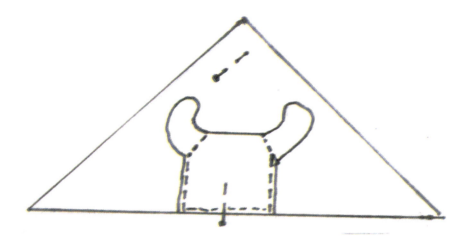

18. Push stuffing in neck opening between pajamas and blanket forming body.

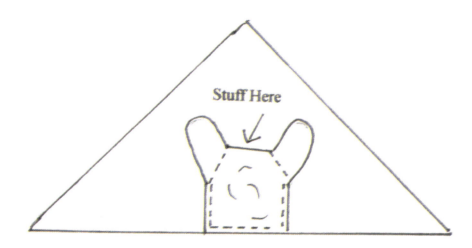

19. Sew top of pajamas closed. If you have a bib, lift up toward top before stitching closed and then lay bib back down.

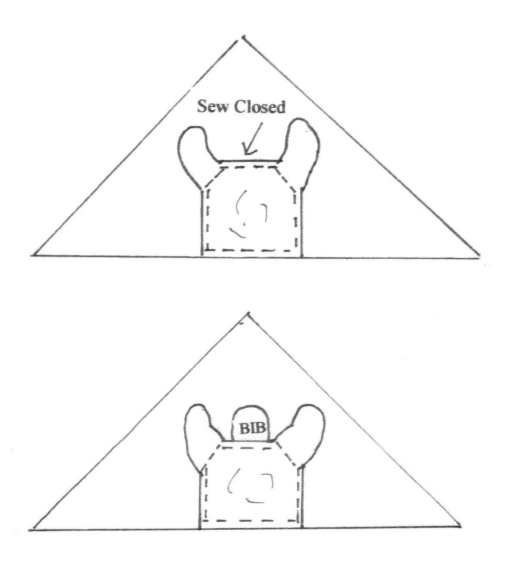

20. TO ATTACH HEAD TO BODY
Pin head in place overlapping chin ½ inch on body as shown on pajama pattern. Pin head securely to TOP layer of blanket or TOP layer of washcloth only.

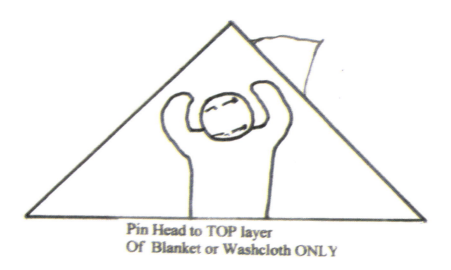

Pin Head to TOP layer
Of Blanket or Washcloth ONLY

21. Using doubled thread hand sew through top blanket or washcloth layer, all around head and center of head, securing head to TOP layer of blanket or washcloth

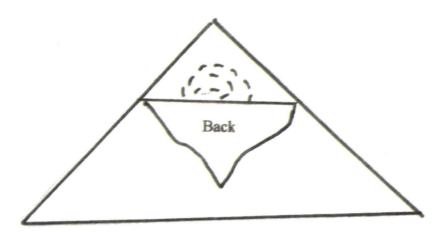

22, Insert needle in seam at back of blanket or washcloth and sew chin in place where chin overlaps body, tacking chin firmly to body. If you have a bib, lay it straight and tack through bib also.

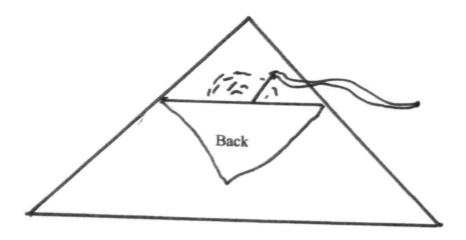

23. Fabric Blanket Only…Baste top points of blanket together. Top Stitch blanket, closing basted edge as you sew.

24. Washcloth Only….Sew from neck to outside edge of washcloth on both sides. Sew top point closed. Leave both bottom sides of washcloth open.

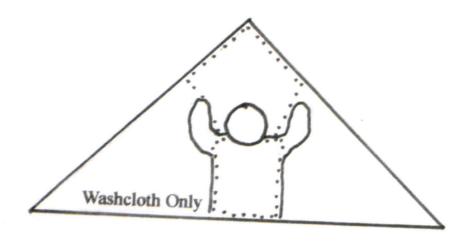

25. Hair Bows or Bow Ties. Sew around leaving open between x's. Clip, turn and press. Gather at center, pull up tight and wrap thread around center three times. Knot off and tack to head or below chin.

26. Do not skip this step—Using brush on blush, pink the cheeks. Or a crayon may be used gently but I prefer the blush. This brings your baby's face alive.

CHOOSE A FACE...Page 1

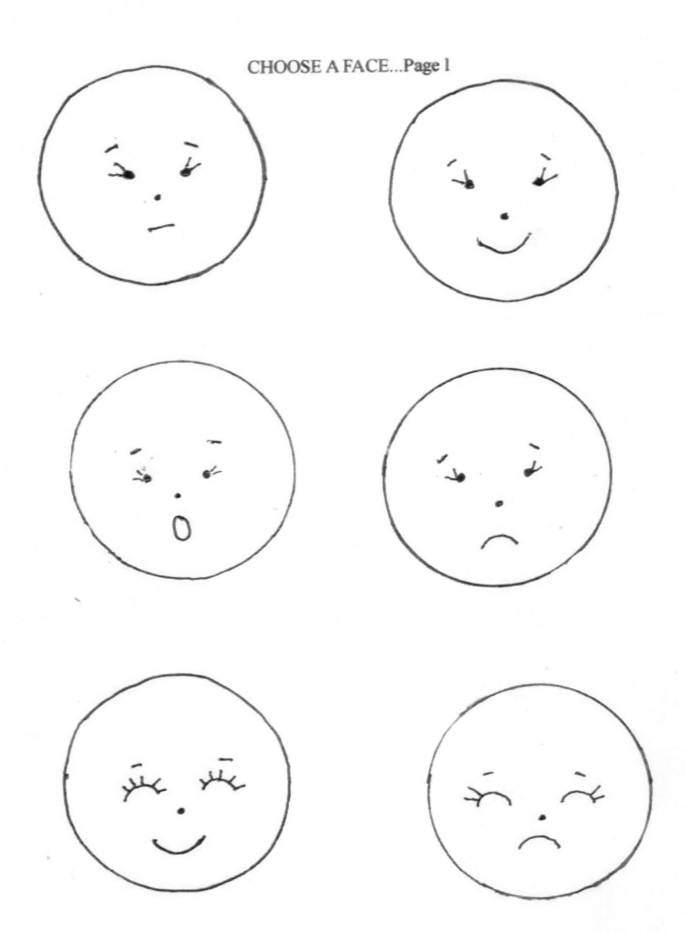

CHOOSE A FACE Page 2

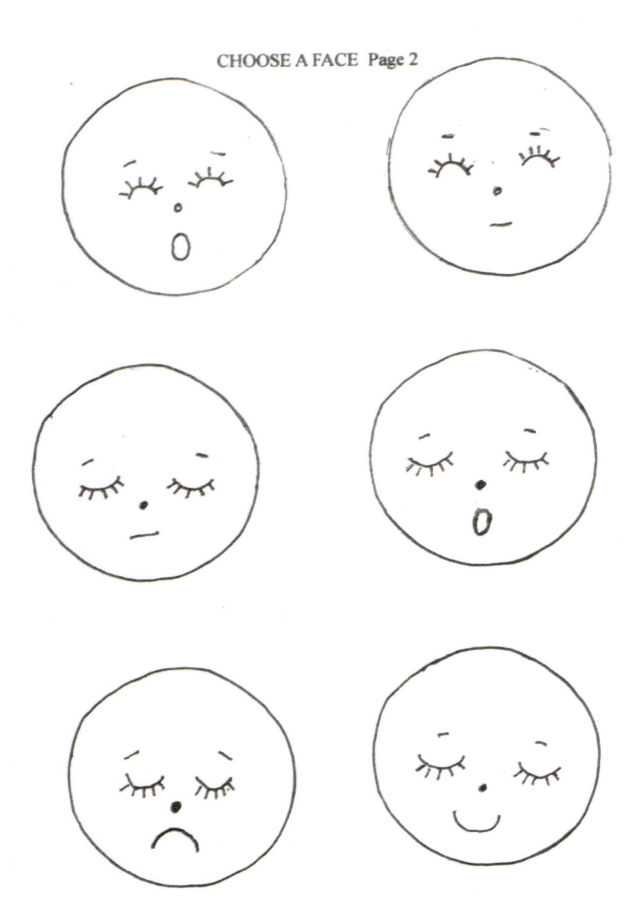

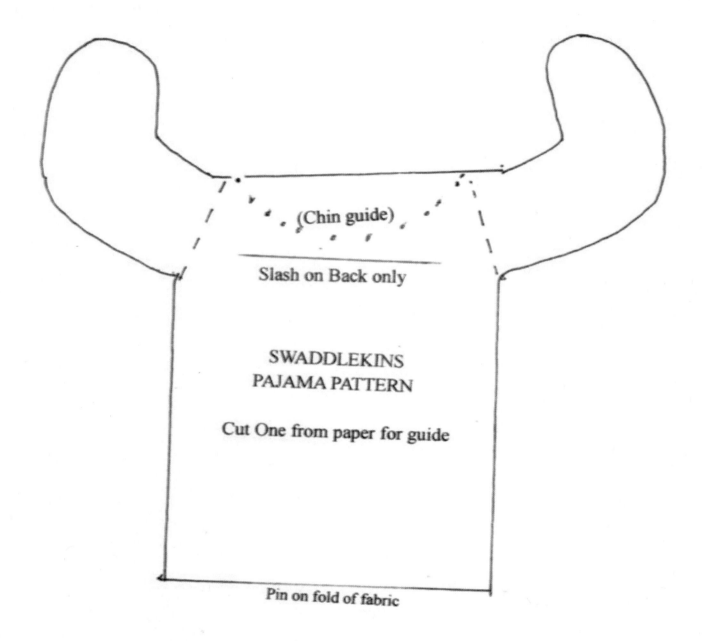

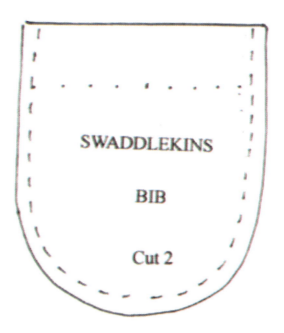
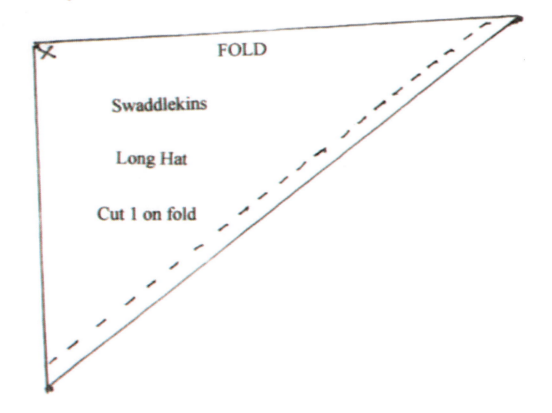

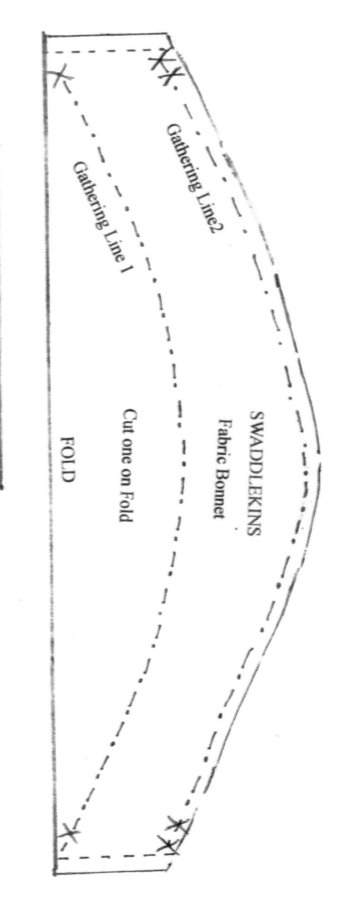
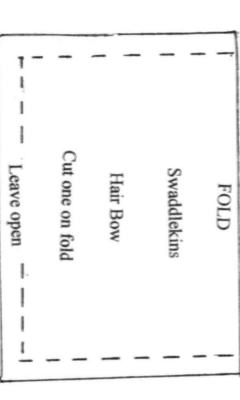

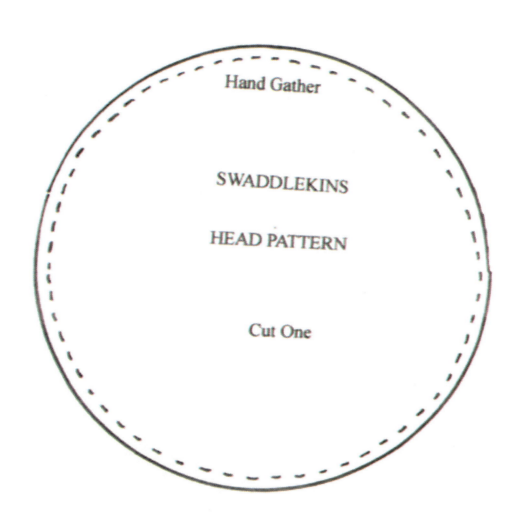

FARM BOY
Sun Hat

Cut one on doubled fabric

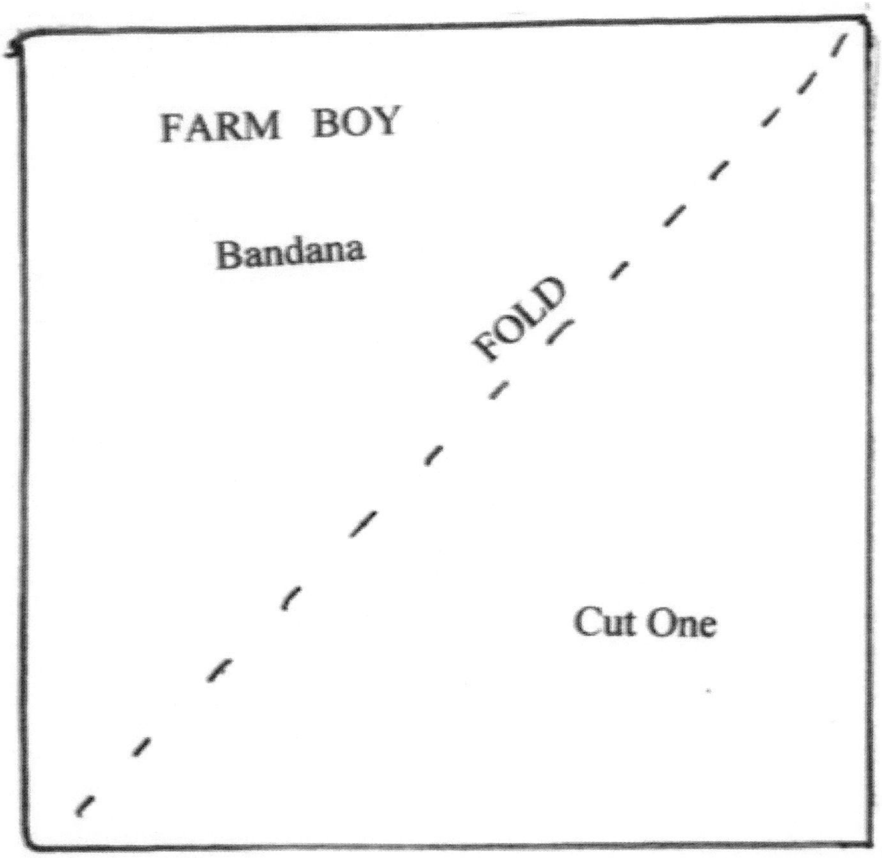

FARM BOY

Bandana

FOLD

Cut One

EMBROIDERED HAIR

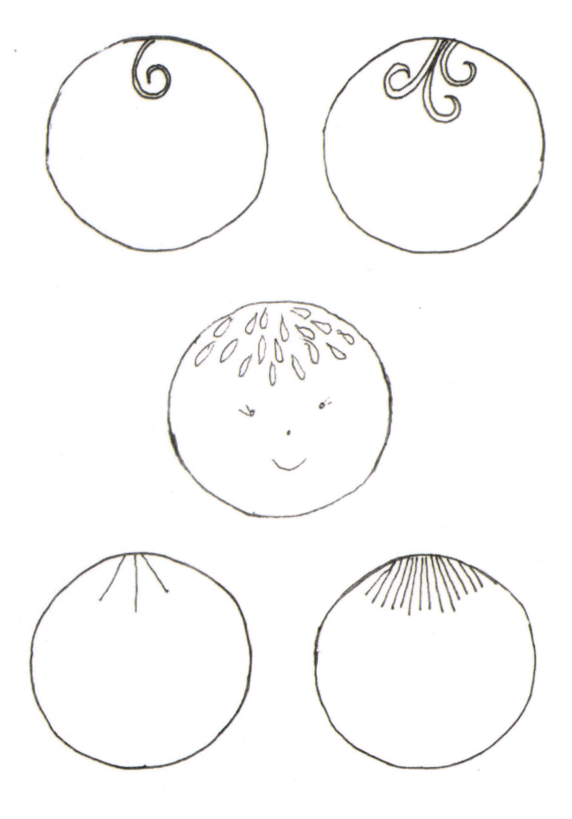

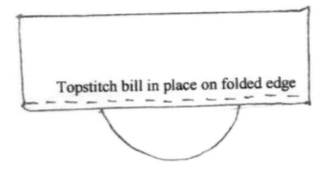

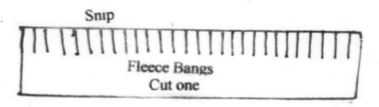

Peekaboo Porch

Easy Cloth Doll PDF Patterns

1021

Froggy Swaddle Baby Doll Pattern

WELCOME TO PEEKABOO PORCH

Come On In and Create with Us....

FROGGY IN A BLANKET SWADDLE BABY

Cuddly 8" Froggy in a Blanket Baby Animal Swaddle Baby Doll Pattern with permanently attached blanket for both boy and girl froggies. Blankets are made with a washcloth in this pattern to make them even quicker and easier. Combine with your favorite fabrics or fabric scraps and colors in any way you choose and create YOUR favorite frog in a blanket! This is a great beginner sewing pattern for cloth animal dolls! Hop to it and start making your Froggy Swaddle Baby Doll today. :o)

Froggy Swaddle Baby

Materials:
- Felt:
    - Two pcs 9 x 12 green felt for head and hands
    - 2-inch x 2-inch scrap of red or pink felt for mouth
    - 1 x 2 inch scrap of white felt for eyes
- Two ¼ inch black, two-hole buttons for eyes
- ¼ yard fabric for pajamas
- One washcloth for blanket
- Polyester fiberfill
- Optional:
    - ¼ yard of ribbon for hair bow or bow tie
    - 7 inches gathered lace for bonnet

Directions:

1. Trace face pattern on paper and cut out. Fold and cut out mouth.

2. Cut two squares of green felt from pattern for head. Fold one layer of felt in half.
3. Fold paper face pattern over folded felt, pin and cut out mouth from felt.

DO NOT CUT OUT THE HEAD YET.

4. Fold other felt piece in half and cut ½" slit in center, making one inch opening when unfolded.

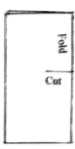

5. Pin pink or red felt under the cut mouth, and using green thread topstitch all around mouth.

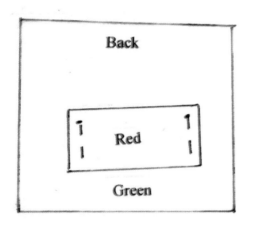 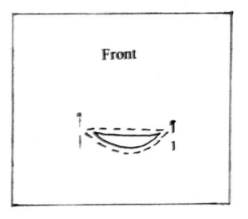

6. Turn over and trim off excess pink/red felt.

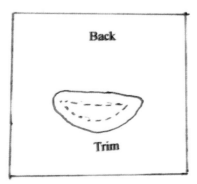

7. Pin paper frog head in place, matching paper mouth to mouth on felt. Using fabric marker or pencil draw around frog head, marking head on felt.

   AGAIN, DO NOT CUT OUT THE HEAD YET.

   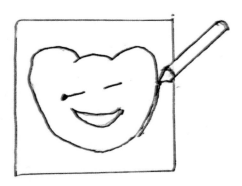

8. Cut two white circles for eyes. (Note: The easiest way to cut small items from felt is to use a sticky note or address label. Draw circle on label side and cut out and remove paper.)

9. Pin eyes in place and slipstich or machine stitch to frog's head on felt layer that has mouth. Sew on black buttons with white thread, forming eye highlights.

Optional: For eyelashes, lift up edge of the white eye circle and make 5 dots with pencil about ¼ inch apart on upper half of eye.

Thread needle with doubled black thread. Insert needle from back of frogs face through dot catching green felt only and not white eye. Pull through leaving a 3 inch tail at back. Use a pencil as guide, wrap thread once around pencil and insert needle back at the same spot you came in.

Pull tight. Tie in back with threaded needle and 3 inch tail knotting 3 times. Then insert needle in green felt only behind eye and knot twice. Be sure to knot into the green felt so eyelashes will stay firm and not slide back. Repeat for each remaining dot.

10. Lay felt square with face up over felt square with slit. Stitch on fabric marker line all around frog's head.

11. Carefully cut out frog's head, leaving a ¼ inch edge.

12. Stuff head with fiberfill through slit in back of head, pushing stuffing up behind the eyes. Stuff head and slipstich the opening closed.

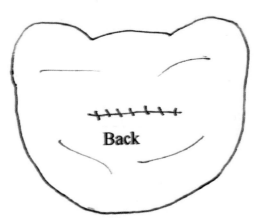

If you want a girl frog with a bonnet, slipstitch gathered lace around back of frog's head now.

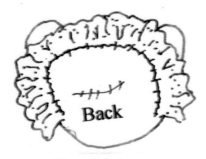

To add Lace

13. Hands – Trace two paper patterns for the hands. Mark all the dots on both paper patterns.

14. Cut four pieces of felt from arm pattern. Pin one paper pattern to two layers of felt. Repeat.

15. Beginning at bottom, sew at edge of paper pattern up the side of the arm to the dot. Sew dot to dot through paper, forming fingers. Sew down the other side of the arm. Follow arrows on figure below for direction.

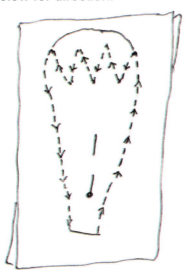

16. Carefully cut out around arm, leaving narrow edge, snipping between fingers to form hands. Remove the paper. (You may have to moisten it to remove it entirely.)

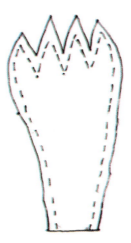

17. Trace pajama pattern and pin to two layers of your pajama fabric, right sides together. Cut out.

18. <u>Only on back layer</u> of pajamas, cut 1-1/2" slit as marked on pattern.

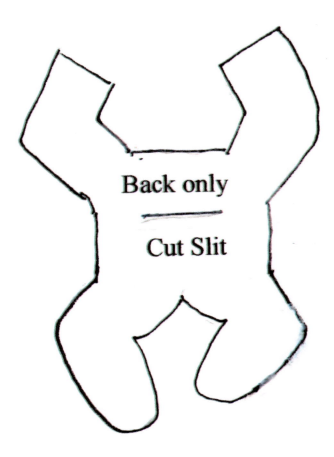

19. Stitch neck from wrist to wrist, right sides together.

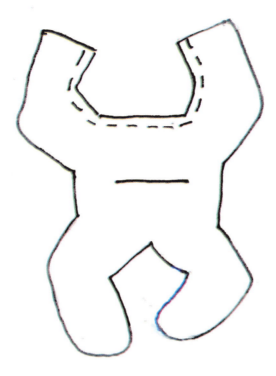

20. Stitch from wrist around the body, legs, and back up to wrist.

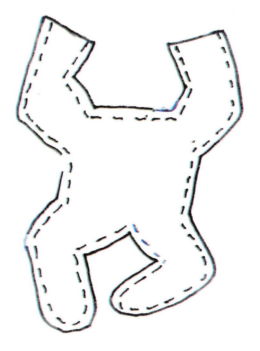

21. Clip all seams carefully and turn right side out through the slit in the back.

22. Fold edge of sleeve under 1/4" at wrist, pushing inside sleeve. Push arm in at wrist, leaving hands out. Sew closed, hemming sleeve and securing arm at the same time.

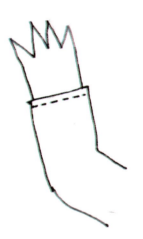

23. Through slit in back of pajamas, push stuffing into arms from wrist to elbow, leaving from elbow to shoulder unstuffed so arm will be poseable and movable.

24. Stuff legs, using eraser end of pencil to push stuffing to toes. Stop at dotted line at top of legs as marked on pajama pattern.

25. Fold washcloth in half, forming triangle. Then fold again and mark center with pin.

26. Pin pajama in place with slit side down on washcloth, matching crotch of frog to pin on washcloth.

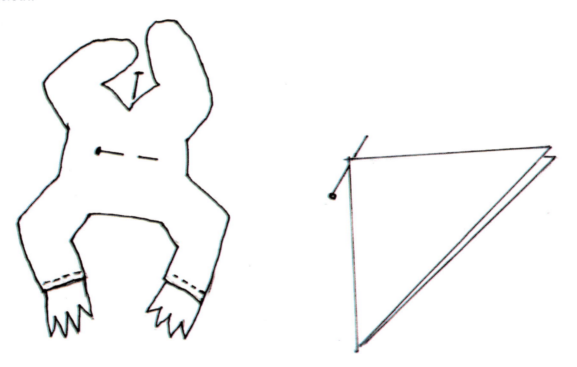

27. Thread sewing machine with color on top to match pajamas and make bobbin thread match the washcloth blanket.

28. Start at top of arm, and following dotted line on pattern, stitch body to washcloth, leaving neck open and arms and legs loose.

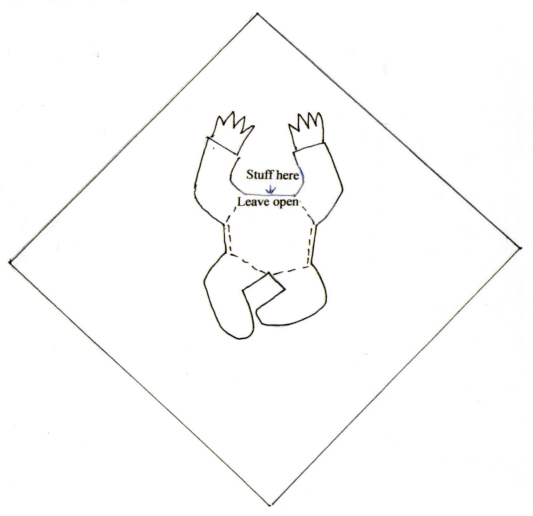

29. Push stuffing in neck between pajama and washcloth blanket, forming body. Sew closed at neck.

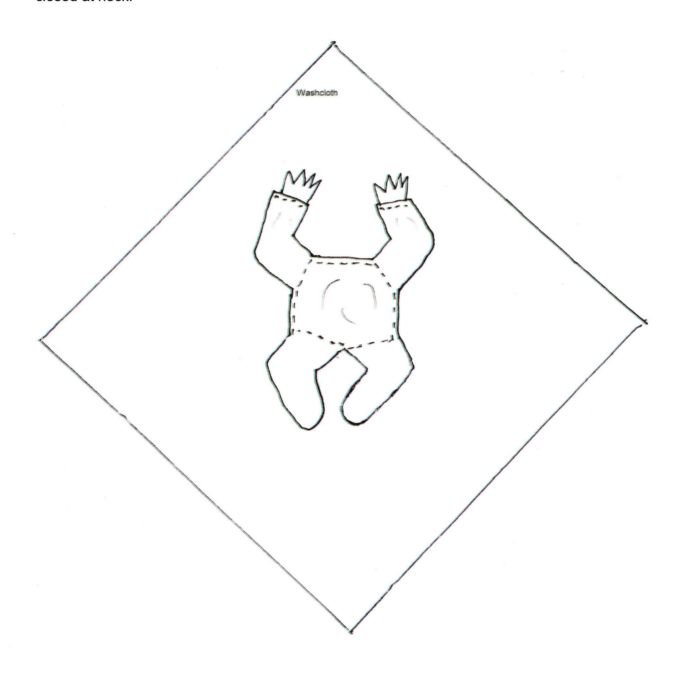

30. Pin frog's head in place, overlapping chin 1/2" on body as shown on pajama pattern.

31. Using doubled thread that matches washcloth blanket, sew frog's head by hand at back of washcloth until firm.

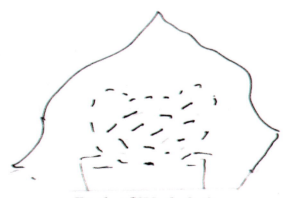

Back of Washcloth

32. Insert needle at neck of pajama, and stitch chin in place until firm, securing chin to body.

33. Add hairbow or bow tie if desired. To make hairbow/bowtie, sew around bowtie pattern, leaving open between Xs. Turn right side out, whipstitch opening closed. Gather in center and sew to frog.

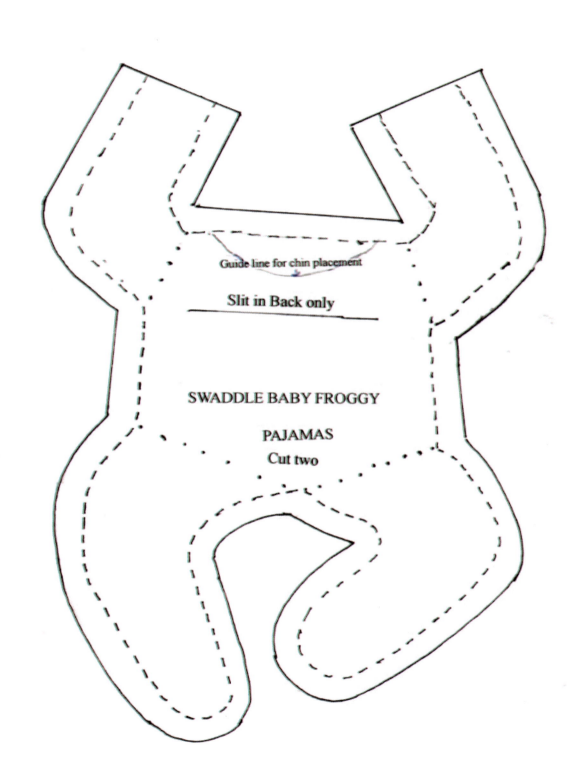

Swaddle Baby Frog

Cut two from green felt
for frog head

Swaddle Baby Frog
Cut four from
green felt for
frog arms

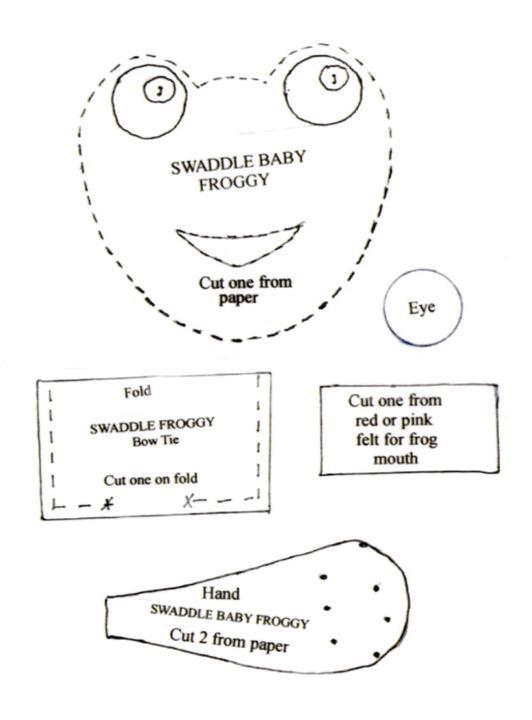

About the Author

Our founder and designer, Jane Bernardo, has been sewing for over 65 years. She has always loved dolls of every shape and size. She began designing doll patterns over 30 years ago and still loves to make new and different dolls whenever she is inspired by her imagination.

If she can imagine it, she can sew it! Feel free to drop her a line or email us a picture of your finished dolls at peekabooporch@gmail.com We would love to hear from you. We hope you enjoy making our patterns as much as we enjoy sharing them with you. Be sure to check out all our patterns on Amazon or visit www.peekabooporch.com

Peekaboo Porch patterns are so much fun,
you can't make just one!

Printed in Great Britain
by Amazon